I AM Creating My Own Relationships

by
Barry Thomas Bechta

**UNCONDITIONAL
LOVE BOOKS**

*Redefining, Guiding, and Inspiring Humanity's
Connection to the Creative Power within.*

I AM Creating My Own Relationships
by
Barry Thomas Bechta

Library and Archives Canada Cataloguing in Publication

Bechta, Barry Thomas, 1968-
   I am creating my own relationships / by Barry
Thomas Bechta.

ISBN 978-0-9686835-3-8

   1. Interpersonal relations--Religious aspects.
2. Spiritual life. I. Title.

BL626.33.B42 2009   204'.4   C2009-905853-7

Publisher's Note

This publication is designed to provide accurate and authoritative information in regard to the subject matter covered. It is sold with the understanding that the author/publisher is not engaged in rendering psychological, legal, or other professional service. If advice or other assistance is required in those areas, the services of a competent professional should be sought.

I AM
Creating My
Own Relationships

I
have a lot
to   remember
about knowing nothing

ACKNOWLEDGMENTS

Relationships are All That Is. I AM always and only in Relationship to All That is.

God/Life/Energy is the Core of my life. My Relationship with God makes my life Whole and Complete. My Core with God forms the basis for all of my Relationships. God is the bullseye in the target of my life. When I hit the bullseye that is God, my Relationships soar in my life.

Next to my Relationship with God, is my Relationship with my Most Cherished Friend, Lover, and Nurturing Partner, Binah. I AM very Grateful that together we define and share our Core Values and Dreams, supporting our individual growth, and Creating a loving supportive family environment.

My two step sons, Anthony and Zachary form the next Relationship level in my life. I welcome their Joy and Growth in my life.

Thank you Clare, Ellen, Melinda, Paul, Sydney, and Gryphon. You are the Greatest Extended Family I could ever desire to have.

Loving thanks to Stephen, Margaret, Gabrielle, and Samuel. With the four of you my Core Principles have been acknowledged, fostered, and loved unconditionally.

I AM grateful to all of the people in my day to day life that help me develop my Relationship with All of God/Life/Energy.

I AM extremely grateful to all the authors that continually inspire me to expand my accomplishments for God, Love, and Life. Thank you Louise L. Hay, Eckhart Tolle, Brock Tully, Mark Victor Hansen, Neale Donald Walsch, Shirley MacLaine, Alan Cohen, Dr. Wayne W. Dyer, Napoleon Hill, Terry Cole-Whittaker, Prince, Robert G. Allen, John Randolph Price, Deepak Chopra, Esther and Jerry Hicks, Marianne Williamson, Jamie Sams, Richard Bach, Joe

Vitale, Helen Schueman and William Thetford.

Once again thank you to everyone who has ever helped me in any way over the years.

I love all of you very much.

TO THE READER

All Relationships are the Perfect Relationships, no matter what appears to be. My Perfect Relationships last:

5 Seconds	Smile/Greet
5 Minutes	Conversation
5 Days	Acquaintance
5 Months	Short Partnership
5 Years	Longer Partnership
5 Decades	Life Long Partnership

Love is a very remarkable thing. I use a bullseye world view for my life. In the centre of my bullseye is my Relationship with God. When I feel Whole and Complete in my Core Relationship with God, my Whole and Complete Core Forms the basis for all of my Relationship Rings. The key to each of my Relationship Rings begins with my Core Relationship with God. Like a pebble thrown into a pond, my Core ripples out into all of my Relationships.

My Relationship Rings

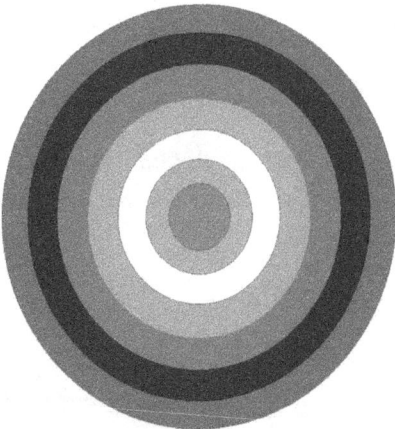

My thoughts and feelings Always Attract all of my Relationships:

1. My Core
2. My Intimate
3. My Family
4. My Friends
5. My Community
6. My Country
7. My World

If I wonder what my Core Beliefs are, I need only look at my Relationship experiences. All of the Relationships in my life mirror my Core Beliefs. Whatever I experience in my life, I believe in my Core without exception. I can Consciously Choose my Core and Consciously Create my Relationship experiences when I understand this.

For many people, Intimate adult Relationships are Challenging. At their Core, these people feel hole and incomplete and therefore Create hole and incomplete Relationships. Only people who feel Whole and Complete in their Cores Create Whole and Complete Relationships.

In my past, when I Chose to be totally honest about my experience and beliefs within my Core, my life Changed drastically. Right Now when I AM Honest about who and what I AM within my Core and share my truth with each Relationship Ring in my life, my life blossoms. When I Choose to do what brings me the most Joy and Connection with God in my Core, I Attract people, places, things, and experiences that mirror my Core. As a result, anything unlike my Core moves away from my experience as well.

All the Love I AM ever going to experience during my entire life, is Present inside of me Right Now. When I Consciously Choose to Open my heart fully to God's Love, the "buzz" of Love is activated as my Joyous feelings. This "buzz" is God/Life/Energy flowing unhindered through me. God/Life/Energy awaits for me to Choose through my Free Will my Open Connection with Love. It is a Choice Only I Can Make. I Choose to Be the Love I AM.

Thank you for being in my Relationship Rings
Barry Thomas Bechta

TABLE OF CONTENTS

I
AM
one cell in
the Body of God

I
AM
one soul in
the Body of God

I AM ONE WITHIN GOD

I AM one cell in the Body of God. I AM one soul in the Body of God. I AM One within God. God is All within me. Without God, I AM not, and without me, God is not. With God, I AM, and with me, God is. God and I are One. I AM God. I AM Grateful for my Oneness within God.

With God, All is possible. God Loves All. God Allows All to Be Fully Free. I AM Fully Free when I AM loving, joyful, and allowing of All That Is. Lasting Freedom is the Freedom I choose within God. Lasting Freedom allows me to Choose all my thoughts, feelings, words, and actions. The Will of God is to BE Free. This is God's Free Will. God is Being Free. I AM Being Free.

God Loves All Unconditionally. Unconditional Love is God's ability to Love all exactly the way it is without needing anything to change. Unconditional Love is God's gift to everyone. Unconditional Love is what God Is and what I AM. God is Unconditional Love. I AM Unconditional Love.

God is always on my side. There is no reason to worry. Everything is Perfect. With God's ever Loving, Abundant, and Successful Nature as my Source and Supply, absolutely everything I Create is Loving, Abundant, and Successful. This truth Manifests in my life through my deepest heartfelt most secret beliefs.

No matter what I believe about my experience, everything is in Perfect Order and Divinely Designed. My belief in anything other than Perfect Order and Divine Design is my belief and my belief alone. It is not the Reality within the Being of God, it is only the reality within my mind. When I Choose that reality in my mind, God can Only Manifest in my experience through what I Choose in my mind.

God is Change. God is Choice. As a cell and soul within the Body of God I AM Change and I AM Choice. I AM Change as I constantly move around the Body of God. All the other parts of the Body of God constantly move as well and I interact with them in ever changing forms. As I interact within the Body of God, I experience new Changes and Choices in each and every moment.

God is Freedom. God is Security. God is Secure in Change.

In my Relationship with God, my security is in knowing that my life is going to change. I AM secure in Change. No matter what experience I AM having Now, it is going to change at some time.

I Choose to foster my Connection with God when my life is in the flow. When my life is in the flow, everything moves well and I have very few worries or concerns. I take time to BE GOD. When I foster and feel my Connection with God, my life blossoms and I AM Blessed. When I AM Grateful for all the Blessings in my life, God provides more and more for me to Accept and Be Grateful for. All of life is like that when I recognise God's Loving Care for me. When things Change and that Change seems too far from where I have been or further from where I desire to go, I can recognise my Connection with God and use that Connection to support me. When I stumble, I fall back into God's Support.

I AM one soul in the Body of God. All of my Relationships radiate in rings out from my Core. My Centre is my Core Relationship with God. Surrounding my Core is my Intimate adult Relationship Ring. The next ring is my Family Ring, followed by my Friend Ring, my Community Ring, my Country Relationships Ring, and then the final Ring Creates my World Relationships.

My strength in all of my Relationship Rings radiates outwards from my Core. My Core Relationship with God is Healthy and Strong through my Chosen Beliefs. I Choose everything I experience. God is All. God is All within me.

I AM ONE WITHIN GOD

*My strength in
all of my Relationship Rings
radiates outwards from
my Core.*

I have a Favourite Rock.
I know nothing about this Rock.
I imagine I know about this Rock.
I think I know about this Rock.
I judge what I imagine and think,
but I know nothing about this Rock.
I only know my own thoughts and
beliefs concerning this Rock.
I can look at this Rock and think
and imagine and judge what I believe,
but that has nothing to do
with the Essence of this Rock.

I AM GOD WITHIN ME

I AM One within God. God is all within me. God is a Rock. I AM a Rock. A Rock needs nothing from anyone. A Rock knows nothing about anyone. A Rock does nothing for anyone. I have a lot to remember about doing nothing, knowing nothing, and needing nothing from anyone or anything but God.

I have a Favourite Rock. I know nothing about this Rock. I imagine I know about this Rock. I think I know about this Rock. I judge what I imagine and think, but I know nothing about this Rock. I only know my own thoughts and beliefs concerning this Rock. I can look at this Rock and think and imagine and judge what I believe, but that has nothing to do with the Essence of this Rock.

My beliefs have nothing to do with any other person, place, or thing either. I can imagine, think, and judge all I want to about any person, place, or thing, but it is impossible to really know anything about those people, places, and things.

This is also true about me. I can imagine, think, and judge all I want to about myself, however this has nothing to do with my Essence. I may imagine, think, and judge myself to be a certain way. This allows me to make up my personality, but that is not the Essence of Who and What I AM. I AM God. I AM Unlimited Freedom and Unconditional Love. I can Choose to Love everything and be Free from everything in every moment of Now. That is Only a Choice I can make.

No matter what I imagine, think, or judge about the Essence of anything, I AM trying to define the indefinable. When I try to do anything, I Choose to Create trying experiences for myself. Instead, I Choose to Create Loving experiences for myself.

The most important Relationship in my life is my Relationship with myself; my Relationship with God within me. When I get this Eternal Internal Relationship to work, all my external Relationships fall into place. Unless and until I take the time to make this Eternal Internal Relationship Full and Free and Loving, my external Relationships suffer because of my false beliefs about Relationships. My external Relationships are an eternal mirror of my internal beliefs concerning Relationships.

I AM Love. I AM Worthy. I Approve of Myself. I AM Self-Respect. Only I can give these to myself. God provides these to me, but I have to Choose them Eternally Internally. The Abundant, Loving, and Successful Energy of God flows eternally through me with all the Love, Worth, Approval, and Respect I could ever desire or need. I AM constantly provided with this. Only I can Choose to Accept this.

I Choose to Accept God's Greatness Oneness Demonstrated when I believe that these qualities are provided by God Ever Present within me. When I look outside of myself for what is Eternally within me, I shut off my Awareness and Access to those very qualities. I AM Choice. I Choose to Accept that I AM inside of myself whatever I seek outside of myself.

When I believe that the world outside of me has more power than the world inside of me, I am unaware. When I am unaware, I can also become angry, depressed, and fearful. Anger, depression, and fear are all triggered by believing in a power other than God. Anger is triggered by the world not being the way I expect. Depression is triggered by low self-esteem. Fear is triggered by worries and worthlessness. All are triggered when I believe in anything other than God.

In my past, when I thought that I knew everything, nothing new happened in my life. When I accepted that I knew nothing, everything new happened in my life. Now I think less to Feel More. I try less to Be more. I talk less to Listen More. I expect less to Perfect More. I am human less to Be God More. I AM One within God.

I AM GOD WITHIN ME

When I thought
that I knew everything,
nothing new happened in my life.

When I accepted
that I knew nothing,
everything new happened in my life.

I am human less
to Be God More.

Hole and incomplete people
Create hole and incomplete Relationships

Whole and Complete people
Create Whole and Complete Relationships

I AM INTIMATE RELATIONSHIPS

I AM One within God. I AM God within me. God is an Orange. I AM an Orange. When I squeeze an Orange I get Orange juice. When I allow the thoughts, feelings, words, and actions of anything outside of me to affect and squeeze me, those experiences bring up whatever is inside My Core.

Intimate Relationships are the ultimate Orange juice maker. More than any other Relationship in my life, Intimate Relationships bring all of my deepest heartfelt most secret beliefs to the surface. Very quickly through my Intimate Relationships, I discover that I AM very good at either being-in-pain or Being-in-Joy. I am either one or the other.

Intimacy reminds me to Choose to Be Unconditional Love, Lasting Freedom, and Open Vulnerability in my Relationships. Whereas lack of intimacy reminds me to Choose to limit my expressions of Love, Freedom, and Vulnerability. Intimate Relationships provide the greatest opportunity for spiritual growth and emotional healing through the mirrors and shadows experienced within committed Intimate Relationships.

God is the heart and soul of my life. God is the centre of my Intimate Relationships. God is the light in my life that illuminates all aspects of my being; those I Choose to acknowledge and those I Choose to ignore. God in the forms of my Intimate Relationships provides the perfect mirrors to illuminate my shadow aspects. What I resist, persists, What I Love, Loves.

God's Presence is the Guiding Love in my life. This Unconditional Love allows me to Love absolutely every person, place, thing, and condition in my life without ever needing to change them. In my past, the things I wished to Change were only my personal shadows I Chose to deny.

With Unconditional Love in my life, I Choose to Be Lasting Freedom and I genuinely express my heartfelt honest celebrations of Love and Joy with others. I Choose personal boundaries rather than impose my personal Choices upon others. I Choose that others have what they wish for in life. I Choose those Core Beliefs for myself as well.

My Intimate Relationships are fuller through the expression of my deepest feelings and through the reception of the deepest feelings of others. My intimacy flourishes when Lasting Freedom is provided for and experienced by Intimate Partners.

In my past, my Intimate Relationships failed because of what I imagined they could provide for me. I went into Relationships looking for what I could not find within myself. I imagined that another person could make me feel loved, or special, or provide me with anything other than what I could give myself. I entered into Relationships as only part of the Complete being I AM. Since Intimate Relationships are mirrors that illuminate my shadows, my Intimate partners are always at the same level of expression that I AM. Hole and incomplete people Create hole and incomplete intimate relationships. Whole and Complete people Create Whole and Complete Intimate Relationships.

I focus on my Core Relationship with God/Life/Energy first. I take the time to understand what I believe I need from others, and heal my Imagined separation from God by Aligning with God within me. My Imagination Creates my Creation. I AM whatever I Imagine.

In my past, a major block to my Intimate Relationships has been my childhood issues and programming. My Intimate Relationships have been affected by what I witnessed as a child. As a result, I Created my Relationship to mirror what I Imagined Relationships were to be like or spent my time denying what I could not bring myself to look at in the mirror of my life.

Now I define and Consciously Choose what I wish for because I Create it. Every thought, feeling, word, and action I make is an act of Creation. When I use all four acts of Creation congruently they Create what I Choose in powerful ways. Just like having a chariot pulled by four horses, when all four horses are going towards the same destination, the arrival time is greatly reduced.

There are two sayings that have impacted my Intimate Relationships in profound ways. The first one is, "If I love someone I can set them free", while the second one is, "I wish for you what you wish for you". Both sayings remind me of Lasting Freedom. I provide Lasting Freedom to myself by providing Lasting Freedom to others.

When I control others, I really only control myself. When I limit others, I really only limit myself. When I Free others, I really only Free myself. When I allow others to experience themselves through who they are Choosing to be, I really only allow myself to experience myself through who I Choose to be. This is Always and Only my Choice. I Choose Lasting Freedom and Wish for everyone that their Dreams come to them.

What I Give to life is what I Live in life. I AM either giving fear or Giving Love to life. I Choose whether I AM being-in-pain or Being-in-Joy. When I give fear to life, I choose to close down my heart to whatever is Now Here. I know I have done this when I feel pain in my life. When I Give Love to life, I Choose to Open my heart up to whatever is Now Here. I know I have done this when I feel Joy in my life. The only thing that is ever Now Here is God/Life/Energy.

Fear closes down, says "no", runs away, harms, curses, creates pain, limits, and feels like a victim in life. Hell is living within fear. Hell is my inability to Love whatever is Now Here.

Love Opens Up, says "YES", Stays Around, Heals, Blesses, Creates Joy, Frees, and Feels Victorious in life. Heaven is living within Love. Heaven is my Ability to Love whatever is Now Here.

I love people because of who I AM, rather than because of who they are. Love is not something that I experience outside of me. Love is ever present within me. All of the love I shall ever experience in my life is Presently within me waiting for me to Access it Consciously.

I feel love for myself within me. I feel Love for others within me. I feel Love from others within me. Everything I feel I only experience within me. I experience absolutely everything within me. I feel more and more Love within me when I Open Up my heart to the Love that flows through me instead of closing down my heart because of fear. I know when my heart is Open because I feel Joy within me.

One area of life that brings up my deepest fears and Love

in Intimate Relationships is Sexuality. In this one area of my life, I have experienced a tremendous amount of growth and healing. I have had to develop habits to replace limited programming from my past. I have had to discover my deepest heartfelt most secret beliefs about sexuality and accept them. In this one area of my life I have felt both being-in-pain and Being-in-Joy.

Sexuality is such an important part of Intimate Adult Relationships, that I define what it means to my life. Sexuality is my experience of physical sensations married with the Presence of Spirit in my life. Sexual lust is dominated by physical sensations, whereas Sexual Love is infused with God/Life/Energy.

My outer world reflects my inner world. No matter what I may be experiencing, those characteristics are Perfect for me to Unconditionally Love them with all my Heart, Mind, and Being.

Whenever I experience large emotional reactions in my Intimate Relationship, I can Choose that experience to deny and destroy, or to Uplift and Encourage Joy and Potential in my life. The most powerful emotional reaction in loving Intimate Relationships is anger for it offers the greatest potential for healing.

Aggressions of anger are destructive and usually directed at particular people, places, and things. Anger that energetically attacks and increases tensions results in pain and separation for all involved. Anger covers up and ignores the pain and fear of separation from God, Love, and Life. All suffering results from a belief in separation from God/Life/Energy.

Expressions of anger, on the other hand, are experienced naturally within healthy Relationships. Expressions of Anger are neutral. They are not directed at any person, place, or thing. Expressions of Anger release energy and relieve tension that builds up. When released in healthy ways, anger expresses the vulnerable healing ability of that energy.

Anger like any other feeling reflects a state of being I have chosen. When I am angry, I have chosen to Be angry. When I am frustrated, I have chosen to Be frustrated. No matter what I am being, I have Chosen to Be exactly that state of Being.

I Commit to Being-in-Joy. I Commit to a new level of healing. I Commit to Create my Core within God as being open, honest, vulnerable, and transparent. I Commit to Conscious Creation. I Commit to Love, Laughter, and Lasting Freedom. I Commit to God and God Commits to me.

I Choose absolutely every state of Being I AM. Intimate Relationships are the perfect mirror to my state of Being. Intimate Relationships can be ruled by fear, limitations, and viciousness, or they can be realised through Love, Freedom, and Vulnerability. Freedom to grow or the Freedom to say "no'. Freedom to give and live the Greatest Feeling of God within me. Freedom to Choose without needing control.

Intimate Relationships provide me with the perfect opportunities to listen. When I take the time to listen to others. I remember to take the time to listen to God every day as well. Listening is a far greater tool in my life compared to talking. When I talk I say the things I imagine work in my life. When I listen I AM One with the things that work in my life. What do I talk most about in my Intimate Relationships? Do I abuse, curse, and criticise my Intimate Relationships? Or do I praise, bless, and compliment my Intimate Relationships? My words convey information as well as my Intention.

Intimate Relationships provide me with the perfect opportunities to forgive. Life is for-giving not for-getting. I can Choose to forget all I know in order to Be all I AM. I can only give what is within me to give. I AM an Orange. Whatever is inside of me gets squeezed into my Intimate Relationships. My Core beliefs makes up the Juice of my life.

Intimate Relationships encourage me to be grateful. Each day is a gift. Each Relationship is a gift. Life is change and the gifts of life change. I have no control over those changes, even though I have infinite choices over my interactions with those changes. I acknowledge the beauty in everyone and everything with gratitude and that is what I continue to Create. I AM One within God. I AM God within me.

I AM INTIMATE RELATIONSHIPS

Fear closes down, says "no", runs away, harms, curses, creates pain, limits, and feels like a victim in life.

Love Opens Up, says "YES", Stays Around, Heals, Blesses, Creates Joy, Frees, and Feels Victorious in life.

I AM FAMILIAL RELATIONSHIPS

I AM One within God. I AM God within me. I AM Intimate Relationships. God is a Ball. There are many different kinds of Balls: basketball, tennis ball, golf ball, etc. There are many different kinds of families: blood relationship, married relations, legal relations, etc. For me any group of people that have a connection and a commitment to the betterment of everyone in the group is a family unit. I AM Parents. I AM Siblings. I AM Children. I AM Relatives. I AM Extended Family.

Healthy Familial Relationships promote Compassion over competition, Betterment of all people rather than being better than some people, a world where the best person helps others, and the first to arrive is the first to help serve others.

Familial Relationships Encourage Open and Honest Communication. Communication that promotes Love and Healing is Fair, Kind, Helpful, Honest, Honourable, Humble, and Respectful. The goal of communication is to Empower everyone, Uplift everyone, and Dignify everyone.

Any thoughts, feelings, words, actions and experiences that promote bad feelings, fighting, frustration, and failure work against a Healthy family environment. Aggravating, denigrating, dominating, frustrating, instigating, and manipulating only create an atmosphere of being-in-pain for everyone concerned.

Every thought, feeling, word, action, and experience that promote Happiness, Harmony, Healing, and Success promote a Healthy family environment. Appreciating, Celebrating, Communicating, Cooperating, Initiating, and Inspiring each other fosters an atmosphere of Being-in-Joy for everyone.

I can only give and receive Love my way. I AM an Orange. When I AM squeezed, I release only what is inside of me. When I AM Whole and Complete, I release that energy to everyone I encounter. When I AM hole and incomplete, I release that energy to everyone I encounter.

Others share their love with me, and no matter what love another shares with me, I can only receive love in a form that matches what is inside of me. When I AM hole and incomplete, I easily receive energy from others that matches my hole and incomplete core. When I AM Whole and Complete, I easily receive energy from others that matches my Whole and Complete Core.

When I feel hole and incomplete inside, I need to do something or anything to fill the emptiness within me. When I feel Whole and Complete, there is nothing I need to do, and I can easily do nothing with my family members and feel Whole and Complete.

Resistance is human. Surrender is Divine. When I Surrender to what is, I Surrender to God. When I resist what is, I am disappointed with what God has brought to me in this moment. This moment brings me the perfect person, place, or thing to Surrender to Love, Life, and God. When I Surrender to the Divine, I Enjoy Being-in-Joy and I AM out of my mind. Whatever I resist, persists. Whatever I love, Loves.

So whether I play basketball with a tennis ball or a baseball or a basketball matters not to God, it only matters to me, until it no longer does. I AM One within God. I AM God within me. I AM Intimate Relationships.

I AM FAMILIAL RELATIONSHIPS

When I feel hole and incomplete inside, I need to do something or anything to fill the emptiness within me.

When I feel Whole and Complete, there is nothing I need to do, and I can easily do nothing with my family members and feel Whole and Complete.

Until I can seek, discover, and praise the divinity in others, I rarely understand the divinity within me.

Accepting others as they are, perfect and divine aspects of God, allows me to accept myself as I AM, a perfect and divine aspect of God.

I AM WORLD RELATIONSHIPS

I AM One within God. I AM God within me. I AM Intimate Relationships. I AM Familial Relationships. God is the World. I AM the World. We are all One. I AM One with all.

Until I can seek, discover, and praise the divinity in others, I rarely understand the divinity within me. Accepting others as they are, perfect and divine aspects of God, allows me to accept myself as I AM, a perfect and divine aspect of God.

Most World Relationships are short lived. Many of them stay only at the first stage and last only 5 seconds. This Relationship is a smile and pleasant greeting. I Choose to put my best self forward in these 5 seconds. I imbue these 5 seconds with The Feeling of God, which can make the difference to another soul in the Body of God. I never know what another requires. I Only know what I require. When I Bless others I Bless myself.

The second stage of World Relationships last 5 minutes. In these Relationships, I smile and greet someone and then I connect with them by exchanging names. My name is the most important word in my world. It is the most important part in another person's world as well. During the rest of this 5 minute Relationship, I listen attentively to whatever another person wishes to share with me. We All Are One. We All just want to be heard. I know that when I share my Dreams, my heart Opens up and my eyes shine with a Light of God's Purpose through me as I talk about my Dreams. So I ask others about their Dreams. In my 5 minute Relationships, I ask others, "What do you love being (rather than doing)? Or, what are your Dreams?" And then I deeply listen and witness other's hearts Open up and eyes shine with the Light of God's Purpose in their life. These 5 minutes Connects both of us to God/Life/Energy.

5 day Relationships take on many shapes and forms: Love, Work, Travel, Education, Spiritual, etc. I have spent 5 days with people and we have shared our deepest sorrows, and I have spent 5 days with people as we shared our greatest Joys. I have experienced great difficultly and great ease in my 5 day Relationships. In these short and intense Relationships, I enjoy being myself with fewer limitations; being Freer and more

Adventurous. Life in 5 day Relationships Creates powerful transformation.

5 month Relationships allow me to Enjoy the ride of life, Relax into the perfection of life, and Express my best self. When I Relax into the perfection of a 5 month Relationship, I know that the perfect people are always coming together in the right way and at the right time. I Enjoy every moment, without worrying about the Relationship. Wherever I place my focus that is what I Create more of. When I Expect Miracles, I Experience Miracles, or grow Miraculously. My 5 month Relationships Provide Lasting Growth that is perfect for everyone involved.

Longer Relationships from 5 years to 5 decades are full of most everything anyone can experience in life. My longest Lasting World Relationships provide me with the perfect opportunities for my growth and healing. All my shadows are provided with experiences to come into Wholeness. All my Light is provided with experiences to shine in Oneness.

Every person, place, and thing in my life is God (Gifts Of Divinity). I AM who I AM with God. I AM who I AM with the World. Everything I AM affects the World. What I think, feel, say, do, and experience may seem like a small drop in the scheme of the entire World, but everything I think, feel, say, do, and experience impacts the World.

In Native Cultures, the World is a family member. Many call the World our Earth Mother. All the life forms on the Earth Mother are our brothers and sisters. Together we form a symbiotic whole where we each affect the other. There is nothing that I do in my part of the world that does not affect the rest of the world. We are totally interconnected. We Are All One. My place in the world either curses or Blesses the entire World.

The collective consciousness of the Earth Mother is contributed to by my consciousness. World Peace or the lack there of is achieved by all my thoughts, feelings, words, and actions combining with absolutely every other person, place, and thing on the Earth Mother. What I believe about the World experience is played out in my experience of the World. What shows up is a mirror of what I believe somewhere inside of me.

We Are All One. I can only see and believe about others, what I Choose to see and believe about myself. I take from others, what I Choose to take from myself. I limit others only in the ways I Choose to limit myself. I give Freedom to others that I Choose to give to myself. When I AM Whole and Complete, my Peace and Tranquillity Blesses the entire world. There is only One. There is only God. There is Only Love. I AM One within God. I AM God within me. I AM Intimate Relationships. I AM Familial Relationships.

I AM WORLD RELATIONSHIPS

Being is an inner world experience.
Doing is an outer world experience.

I AM BEING THE SOURCE

I AM One within God. I AM God within me. I AM Intimate Relationships. I AM Familial Relationships. I AM World Relationships. God is the Source of all that is. I AM the Source of all that is. Everything that God is, I AM.

I AM the Source. No matter what I wish to Be, I AM the Source of that Beingness. I AM Being the Source. When I desire to experience Love in all its fullness, I AM the Source of my experience of Love in all its fullness.

I can only give and receive love my way. I perceive my entire experience within me. I may imagine that I am acting in the outside world, but that is only my perception. My entire world experience takes place within me.

When I think a thought, it takes place within my being. When I feel a feeling, it takes place within my being. When I say a word, I perceive it within my being. I may describe that a sound is outside of my body, but the actual perception always occurs within my being. Everything I think, feel, say, act, and experience, I perceive within my being.

I AM the Source and Supply of my Perception. All my thoughts, feelings, words, and actions take place within me. The entire scope of my experience occurs within my heart, mind, and being. There is only me. I AM All That Is.

Being is different from doing. Doing is a result of Being, Being is The Cause of Doing. Being is an inner world experience. Doing is an outer world experience.

I Choose to do something. The something that I do is a means to an end. I Choose to do the dishes. Doing the dishes is a Choice I make in the hopes of producing a Beingness experience. I may do the dishes, so that I can Be helpful. However doing the dishes may not Be helpful when doing the laundry is required.

In life I Choose a whole host of Doing activities in the hopes of producing Beingness experiences. I go out with a person in the hope of Being Happy. I go to work in the hopes of Being Abundant. I sleep in late in the hopes of Being Rested. I do the dishes in the hopes of Being Helpful. I talk kindly with someone in the hopes of Being Friendly.

Doing all these different things, in my outer experience, sometimes provides me with the Beingness states I desire to experience, but it does not guarantee them. The only thing that can guarantee those states is to Choose to Be a particular state of Beingness within me in whatever experience is Present.

In my inner world, when I Choose to Be Happy, that Beingness state is Created. When I Choose being Happiness, I very quickly notice that something in my outer experience challenges my inner state of Beingness. I AM provided with a Choice to continue Choosing to Be happy or Be another state of Being.

In every single moment I AM Choosing to Be something. When I AM Happy, I AM Choosing to Be Happy. When I AM Angry, I AM Choosing to Be Angry. No matter what I AM Being, I AM Choosing to Be exactly that State of Being in every moment of Now.

I have all the Choice and all the Control over my states of Being. Controlling the people, places, things, and experiences in the external world is a losing battle once I start down that road. Controlling what I AM Being in my internal world is a winning journey once I Choose to Be Free.

In every moment I AM presented with a new choice. The illusion of life is imagining that my doing experience in my external world is what produces my Being experience in my internal world. The truth is that my Being experience in my internal world produces my doing experience in my external world.

When I Choose particular Dreams of experience in my external world; when I Do things I imagine will give me States of Being I wish to live, these activities rarely produce my State of Being. No matter what is externally happening, it can only affect my Beingness if I Choose that it can. I AM always the Source of my Beingness. I AM Being the Source.

I AM the Source of all that I wish to experience.

That single wonderful statement challenged me for years to embody and Consciously Create my experience. I imagined that

Being the Source of all I wished to experience Created particular forms. Being the Source is a feeling experience. When I struggle for particular forms my feelings support a hole and incomplete struggle. When I AM Whole and Complete my feelings support Whole and Complete Success. I AM the Source of All I Choose to experience.

When I Choose to experience loving and nurturing Relationships in my outer world, I know I AM the Only One who can Align with, Allow, and Accept them into my life. In my past, I imagined that I had to Be Loving and Nurturing to all in my experience, but I only need to Be Loving and Nurturing in my inner world. I release my need to interact with the illusions outside of me to Create experiences in my life.

When I Choose to Be Loving and Nurturing in my inner world, everything but Loving and Nurturing is mirrored in my outer world, reminding me to Choose Loving and Nurturing. I Choose to Love and Nurture myself within my Core for the experience of Being Whole and Complete. When I AM Whole and Complete, I may Choose to leave a situation, I may Choose to ignore a situation, or I may Choose to confront a situation. Whatever Choice I make allows me to Be Loving and Nurturing within my Core Relationship with God/Life/Energy.

If my challenging experience is a Relationship, I may Choose to leave the Relationship with the full knowledge that the Beingness State within me has not changed and follows me into my next Relationship. When my inner Beingness State stays constant, my outer experience stays constant even with new people.

The more I feel Whole and Complete in my inner world, the more I AM Whole and Complete in my outer world. It is not my journey to live life for another person, nor to allow another to live mine. It is not my purpose to be domineering over others, nor to be a door mat to others. Freedom to be and choose with God/Life/Energy the best feeling choice I can is my purpose. Sometimes that self Aware choice poses challenges in relationships. I Align with, Allow, and Accept God as my Core. I AM Being the Source of that which I seek.

I AM the Source of my Abundance. When I Choose to Be

Abundant, everything that does not support my Abundance appears to come into my outer world experience. I let my outer experience, be what it may, and I focus on being Abundance in my inner world. My experience is only perceived through me. My experience is only received through me. My Abundance is present within me. Abundance can fluctuate in the illusions of my outer experience, but it is ever present within my Being. I AM The Source of my Abundance.

All the Love, Success, Abundance, Peace, Health, and Joy I shall ever experience in my entire life currently resides within me and awaits my Choice to Consciously Align with, Allow, and Accept God/Life/Energy to Manifest in my experience.

I AM the Source of my Miracles. I Choose to Be Miraculous. When I Choose that state of Being, the exact opposite comes into my experience. The exact opposite of miraculous is Expected or Normal. It is an easy illusion of life to experience miracles as expected and normal in my outer world. I AM One within God. I AM God within me. I AM Intimate Relationships. I AM Familial Relationships. I AM World Relationships.

I AM BEING THE SOURCE

I Choose to Be Miraculous.
When I Choose that state of Being,
the exact opposite comes into my experience.
The exact opposite of miraculous is expected or
normal. It is an easy illusion of life to
experience Miracles as expected
and normal in my outer world.

Resistance is human.

Surrender is Divine.

I Enjoy Being~in~Joy.

I AM out of my mind.

I AM HEALING

I AM One within God. I AM God within me. I AM Intimate Relationships. I AM Familial Relationships. I AM World Relationships. I AM Being the Source. God is a Field of Feeling. My experience of God is as a Being within that Field of Feeling. My Feelings are infinite within that Field of Feeling.

Feelings are experienced in the present moment. Emotions are Feelings from past moments in the present moment. Emotions are different from Feelings. Emotions are Feelings with a story. When emotions enter my present experience, there is a story that needs to be healed. A belief in the story that I have Created accepts a belief in my separation from all of Love, Life, and God. The only thing that can separate me from all of Love, Life, and God is my own thoughts.

When my inner Being, Feels something, my inner Being Creates my outer experiences from that Feeling. When my Feeling is wrapped in a story, my inner Being Creates my outer experience from that story. My stories cloud my ability to Be fully in the present moment.

When I Feel hurt because of an experience from my past, my present feeling is not a Free Feeling experience. My present becomes a fixed feeling experience. Fixed feeling experiences are fixed to repeat what was felt in the past. Free Feeling experiences are Free to Feel whatever state of Being in the Present I Choose.

My ego loves fixed feeling experiences because they are the same. They are something I have felt before and I understand them. No matter how uncomfortable a fixed feeling experience may be, I AM comfortable with them because I have felt them before. Fixed feelings experience are accessed by my ego, my emotionally guided opinions.

The voice of God, on the other hand, is the voice within me that Gives Ongoing Direction. The voice of God suggests that I can Be Free Feeling in the present moment - Feeling Free from my past, Free from my limits, Free from my expectations, Free for my perfection.

Anger in and of itself is an incredible Free Feeling Energy.

It can powerfully be used in the present moment. However anger is one Free Feeling that can become trapped within my emotional Being as a fixed feeling. Anger is a powerful healing tool when it's expression lifts me out of feeling powerless. When it's expression reinforces a memory loop of pain, my anger keeps me powerless.

Pain can be hidden by many things. Anger hides pain. Depression hides pain. Apathy hides pain. Addictive behaviours hide pain. Any addictive behaviour is a behaviour that seeks to separate me from my pain. Addictive behaviours include any thing used excessively to ignore my hole and incomplete feelings. I could use sex, drugs, alcohol, food, work, reading, shopping, or any other activity to deny my pain within hole and incomplete feelings.

All addictive behaviours mask painful emotions. All painful emotions stem from a Choice on my part to separate myself from God in my past. This choice may be conscious or unconscious. I can make a new Free Feeling Choice concerning my Unity with God. When I recognize that my very strong emotional opinions and my addictive behaviours are masking my pain, I can access the doorway to my Healing.

When I AM Feeling, I AM Healing. Whatever I AM Feeling provides the perfect opportunity for my Healing in the present.

All strong emotional reactions and addictive behaviours mask my pain. When I feel hole and incomplete, my fear appears along with my pain, my emotional opinions, and my addictive behaviours.

When I feel worthy of Life, Love, and God, I feel Whole and Complete and I have Faith that all I need is provided for me. As a result, my fear, my pain, and my emotional opinions, and my addictive behaviours fall away when I no longer energize them.

Resistance is human. Surrender is Divine. I Enjoy Being-in-Joy. I AM out of my mind. When I AM out of my mind, I forget my stories. When I AM out of my mind, I forgive my stories. In my inner world, anything other than The Feeling of God is just stories.

When my stories are forgotten, my ego (emotionally guided opinions) screams that I MUST be, do, or have particular people, places, and things in my life because I win with them or lose without them, but Free Feelings naturally follow the voice of God (Giving Ongoing Direction) that says that I can be, do, have people, places, and things in my life just for the experience of them.

When I AM Free Feeling, I AM Freely Healing. I AM Appreciation. I AM Celebration. I AM Communication. I AM Compassion. I AM Cooperation. I AM Feeling. I AM Forgetting. I AM Forgiving. I AM Freedom. I AM God. I AM Guiltless. I AM Harmless. I AM Harmony. I AM Healing. I AM Helpful. I AM Humble. I AM Initiation. I AM Innocence. I AM Listening. I AM Motivation. I AM Unconditional Love. I AM Understanding. I AM Wisdom and Clarity. I AM One within God. I AM God within me. I AM Intimate Relationships. I AM Familial Relationships. I AM World Relationships. I AM Being the Source.

I AM HEALING

I AM Responsible for absolutely everything in my life, Absolutely Everything, without exception.

My Responsibility is for absolutely everything in my life, not any one else's life.

I AM Absolutely Responsible for my life, my inner Choices, my inner Changes, and my inner Control.

I AM RESPONSIBILITY

I AM One within God. I AM God within me. I AM Intimate Relationships. I AM Familial Relationships. I AM World Relationships. I AM Being the Source. I AM Healing. I AM Responsible for absolutely everything in my life, Absolutely Everything, without exception.

Being Responsible for Everything in my life means exactly that. I AM Responsible for all the good and all the bad. There is no good or bad, there is only my perception of *What Is. What Is* may be perceived as good if it works in my life, and it may be perceived as bad when it does not work. No matter What Is, *What Is* is perfect.

The Perfection in every moment of Now is a result of the Universe Being Change. Everything Changes. God Changes. I Change. Experiences Change. There is nothing that does not Change, except for the concept of Change. In every moment of Now, I AM presented (gifted) with a moment of Choice. In every moment of Choice, I have all the Control over my inner Choice and Change.

I AM Responsible for absolutely everything in my life, Absolutely Everything, without exception. My Responsibility is for absolutely everything in my life, not anyone else's life. I AM Absolutely Responsible for my life, my inner Choices, my inner Changes, and my inner Control.

Responsibility is my Ability to Respond to my Changes, my Choices, and my Control. I can only Control my inner state of Being. When I concern myself with Changes, Choices, and Control outside of me, I have placed my attention on anything other than the Feeling of God within me. When I Choose to Control my focus and Change its placement from external people, places, and things to place it on the Eternal internal Feeling of God within me, my inner world becomes my Chosen state of Being and my outer world reflects my Choice.

When I AM Responsibility, I take Control of my thoughts, feelings, words, and actions and Choose to Change them from anything external and place them towards everything Eternal.

When I AM Responsibility, I AM Respectful. Being Respectful is Choosing to Be full of Respect. Respect is an inner journey or Choice, Change, and Control. Others cannot provide me with Respect. Others only mirror my inner belief in Respect. When my outer experience is without Respect, I can Choose to Change and Control my inner beliefs about Respect.

I AM Aware of my State of Being. My strong emotional opinions are doorways to my healing. I AM Internal Choice, Change, and Control. I allow my pain to access my healing energy immediately. I AM Unconditional Love and Lasting Freedom. I Yield to God's Eternal Guidance and Support.

In my external world, yielding can mean giving to others or giving into others. In my past, I have Yielded to others because I imagined my yielding would produce the desired result of getting what I imagined I could only get through yielding to others.

In my internal world, Yielding to God, allows me to access the Abundance, Love, and Successful nature of God Naturally residing within me. I Now realize that The Power of God is constant within me. I take Responsibility for my life. I accept that my Power comes only from within me.

Because everything in my outer world experience mirrors my inner world beliefs, I AM Responsible for Absolutely Everything I experience. When I experience a lack of love from individuals around me, I recognise that my love vibration for others around me is lacking. What I Give is what I live. If I give boundlessly of my love to others without condition, boundless amounts of love come to me without condition. Whatever I access as the Core of my Love, becomes my experience of Love.

My deepest heartfelt most secret beliefs about Love are what I truly share with others, project upon others, and experience in return from others. There is no exception. What I resist, persists. What I love, Loves. What I Give, Lives.

Nowhere is this more apparent that within myself. When I truly love myself and exude self-love and worthiness, every experience I have with others mirrors my inner beliefs of self-love, worthiness, respect, and Responsibility.

I AM Responsible. I AM Worthy. I AM Choice. What I

AM internally is reflected in my world externally. I AM true to myself. I AM One with the Feeling of God within me. I express from my Core.

I AM One within God. I AM God within me. I AM Intimate Relationships. I AM Familial Relationships. I AM World Relationships. I AM Being the Source. I AM Healing.

I AM RESPONSIBILITY

What I Resist, Persists.

What I Love, Loves.

What I Give, Lives.

I AM TRANSPARENCY

I AM One within God. I AM God within me. I AM Intimate Relationships. I AM Familial Relationships. I AM World Relationships. I AM Being the Source. I AM Healing. I AM Responsibility. I AM Truth. I AM Vulnerability. I AM Transparency.

Transparency is my Choice to be Open about absolutely everything in my life. I share my truth with everyone every time about everything. Being Vulnerable and Opening my heart to all in my experience is an incredible journey.

Being Vulnerable with my Heart can allow painful experiences. Fear is the cause of all pain. Fear is the cause of all physical, mental, emotional, and spiritual pain. Fear is a belief in limitations. Fear is a Choice I can make about something that has not happened yet. Fear lives in secrets and lies.

Love is Transparent. Love is limitless. Love is a Choice. Love is a Choice not a result. Love is a Choice I can make about something that has not happened yet. Love is the cause of all physical, mental, emotional, and spiritual pleasure. Love is Transparent. Everything about Love is crystal clear. Love lives through Openness and Honesty.

In all Relationships, Love is a Choice I can make before anything even happens. I Can Choose to Love someone else because of Who and What I AM. When I AM God, I AM Abundant, Loving, and Successful. When I AM Abundant, Loving, and Successful, I AM Whole and Complete and I need nothing from outside of me. I Love and Accept what is offered to me when it matches my Core, because I AM Abundant, Loving, Successful, Whole, and Complete.

Love that is Pure and True never damages, abuses, or takes advantage of people, places, or things. Love that is Pure and True is constantly supplied by the Source and Supply within. It is Constant, and without need. This Love is Transparent. The intent of Love is Apparent and Obvious. There is nothing that is uncertain about love that is Pure and True.

Fear feels hole and incomplete. Fear results from a lack of

clarity. Fear manifests as a lack of love. Fear speaks through pain and punishments. Punishments artificially limit Freedom.

Full and Complete Transparency is without pain and without punishments. Consequences in my life naturally result from my Choices. Every Choice I make results in natural consequences. In my past, I made Choices and ignored the natural consequences and was surprised by any pain (which I pretended to myself was unexpected) when those consequences showed up. Now I AM Transparency. Transparency is Wholly Aware and Completely Responsible.

The greatest illusion of life is limitations. Limitations are my belief in what appears to be on the surface rather than transparently seeing through the illusions. God is absolutely all that is. There are no limits in the Being of God. God is All. Limitations only exist in the mind of humans. Illusions only exist in the mind of humans. Freedom and Reality exist in the Mind of God.

Humans can limit the Freedom and Reality of life by closing down the access door to Abundance, Love, Success, Peace, Health, and Joy. The access door is always unlocked and available to be opened. When I feel Whole and Complete, I easily Align with, Allow, and Accept God's Power into my life. When I feel Whole and Complete with God, I AM.

The Reality of life is Abundant, Loving, and Successful. The Transparency of life is Abundant, Loving, and Successful. I AM One within God. I AM God within me. I AM Intimate Relationships. I AM Familial Relationships. I AM World Relationships. I AM Being the Source. I AM Healing. I AM Responsibility.

I AM TRANSPARENCY

Consequences in my life
naturally result from my
Choices. Every Choice I make
results in particular consequences. In my
past, I made Choices and ignored the natural
consequences and was surprised by any pain
(which I pretended was unexpected)
when those consequences Manifested.
Now I AM Transparency.
Transparency is Wholly Aware
and Completely Responsible.

Within the Being of God, there is the experience of
Free Will of Choice and Control
over my inner world.

Within my inner world, I may believe in anything
other than the Abundant, Loving, and
Successful Nature of God.

It is always my Choice over which
I have total Control.

I AM UNCONDITIONAL LOVE

I AM One within God. I AM God within me. I AM Intimate Relationships. I AM Familial Relationships. I AM World Relationships. I AM Being the Source. I AM Healing. I AM Responsibility. I AM Transparency.

God is Unconditional Love. God's Unconditionally Abundant, Loving, and Successful Energy goes to absolutely everything in existence. Every person, place, and thing in the Being of God receives God's Abundant, Loving, and Successful Energy in the exact same way. Every cell/soul within God is Abundant, Loving, and Successful through each cell/soul's Choices.

Within my inner world, I may Believe in anything other than the Abundant, Loving, and Successful Nature of God. It is always my Choice. I Consciously Choose God/Life/Energy.

Unconditional Love is a journey within God. The opposite of Unconditional Love is conditional fear. Conditional fear is a journey without God. In reality, a journey without God is impossible, for God is all of Life. Everything in existence is a part of the Being of God. Notwithstanding a cell/soul within the Being of God can Choose of its own free will to go without the Abundant, Loving and Successful Power of God. In my past, I have Chosen to be without God and I have Chosen to be with God.

My Relationship with God is Whole and Complete, I have access to all of God's Abundant, Loving, and Successful Energy. God's Unconditional Love envelops me in warmth and says through me, "I Choose what is best for myself".

God constantly supplies all I need in my journey of life. Most of the time, there is nothing I need. There are many things I may want, desire, and lust after, but there is nothing I need that is not provided. In this very moment, I AM Provided for. God Provides all I need for my experience of all of Life, Love, and God.

What do I need right Now to Open to All That Is Right Here Right Now? God is Unconditional Love. What I need and what God is for every person, place, thing, and experience in my life is Unconditional Love. What if I need Money to pay the rent today or I will be removed from my home. God provides whatever is needed when it is needed, not a moment sooner. What is needed in every situation is Unconditional Love.

When I AM Working towards my Dreams in life, they seem to take a very long time. However they take exactly the amount of time they need to take wherein all the pieces are in place to produce the result that matches my deepest heartfelt most secret beliefs about my Dreams. Whether my Dreams and needs are associated with money, health, creative self-expression, or Relationships, God Always in All Ways provides what is needed - Unconditional Love.

Everything comes to me in the right way and at the right time for my deepest heartfelt most secret beliefs. Not a moment sooner. When I AM Whole and Complete, so are my desires, and they allow me to experience my fullest beliefs in all of Love, Life, and God at that very moment. I can only experience Love, Life, and God through my inner beliefs of Love, Life, and God. Nothing more. Nothing less. I experience whatever I AM Able to imagine in my experience.

I AM One within God. I AM God within me. I AM Intimate Relationships. I AM Familial Relationships. I AM World Relationships. I AM Being the Source. I AM Healing. I AM Responsibility. I AM Transparency.

I AM UNCONDITIONAL LOVE

Everything comes to me in the right way and at the right time for my deepest heartfelt most secret beliefs.

Not a moment sooner.

When I AM Whole and Complete, so are my desires, and they allow me to experience my fullest beliefs in all of Love, Life, and God at that very moment.

I can only experience Love, Life, and God through my inner beliefs of Love, Life, and God.

Nothing more. Nothing less.

I experience whatever I AM Able to imagine in my experience.

I AM Love and Compassion

Do I feel hate, anger, and frustration?
Yes, I Create pain through my concentration.
Do I fight to be right over Choosing to be happy?
Yes, God's Giving Ongoing Direction away from crappy.
Do my thoughts, feelings, words, and actions bitterly attack?
Yes, my deepest heartfelt most secret beliefs always come back.
Do I enjoy my experience of pain over Abundant Joy?
Yes, only I can Choose to play with frustrating toys.
Do I realize that I AM the Co-Creator?
Yes, I AM Love and Compassion.
Yes, I AM the instigator.

Thank You God

I AM LOVE AND COMPASSION

The poem on the previous page is a reminder for me when I feel separate from All That Is. The greatest separation in my experience occurs when I fight with others in my experience. I have experienced terrible fights with the people I love the most. In all my fights, I have been at cause in my Choice of separation. In all my fights, I have been at cause in my Choice of needing to have my expectations met.

I would now like to talk in more detail about the poem to remind myself of the Creative power within the clarity of my Choices whether they are Conscious or unconscious.

Do I feel hate, anger, and frustration?

I Choose my feelings always in all ways. I would love to access more peace, joy, and tranquillity in my experience. The way to access more peace, joy, and tranquillity is by accepting all my feelings.

Sometimes I feel hate, anger, and frustration in my experience. Sometimes I feel worry, fear, and uncertainty. Everything I feel is there for me to Accept with Love and Compassion. Anything I resist, persists. Anything I deny, I rely upon in my experience. Anything I Love, Loves in my experience.

When I feel my hate, anger, and frustration, I become Aware of it. When I AM Aware of my hate, anger, and frustration, I can be Honest about its presence in my experience. When I AM Honest about its presence, I can take Responsibility for my feelings and my experience.

I Create pain through my concentration.

When I AM Responsible, I realize that only I Create my experience through all I put into motion. When I put something into motion by Choosing it, I concentrate it onto myself. Sometimes I imagine that pain is something that occurs to me, without realizing that all pain is something Only I can Choose to Create. I can Consciously Choose to Create pain or Joy. It is always my Choice and God provides for me whatever I Choose.

God is a field of Limitless Potential. God's Limitless Potential is accessed by all my thoughts, feelings, words, and actions. God constantly showers Limitless Potential onto All That Is. All That Is Chooses whatever part of that Limitless Potential the All That Is Chooses to experience Now. God gives me the Choice. I can Choose whatever I wish.

In my past, because of my human experiences it has been easy to believe in pain over Abundant Joy. However, I AM able to Concentrate my thoughts, feelings, words, and actions in any way I Choose. Anything I concentrate upon becomes my reality.

I AM Grateful I have Created boundaries to my Limitless Potential (in the human experience) as I learn to access God's Limitless Potential. I AM Grateful that my experience has led me to where I AM Now to fully and Consciously Access the Limitless Potential of God.

Do I fight to be right over Choosing to be happy?

Every fight I experience in my life stems from my firm belief that I am right and the other person is wrong. This belief allows me to perceive I am right and at the same time allows me to immediately receive the experience of how very wrong I feel through my Chosen belief.

Yes, God's Giving Ongoing Direction away from crappy.

Every fight provides the perfect opportunity for me to realize I AM Choosing to fight and Choosing to feel crappy. It is always my Choice about what I wish to experience. I Choose to release my crappy beliefs and express happy beliefs. I Choose to Create win-win situations for All That Is.

The resistance I experience with another person is God Giving Ongoing Direction to find a different way and a simpler way which allows me to be happy and allows everyone to feel empowered through their Choices.

Do my thoughts, feelings, words, and actions bitterly attack?

When I forget my place in the Conscious Creative Cycle, I use all my thoughts, feelings, words, and actions to bitterly attack the people, places, and things in my experience. In my past, when I have completely forgotten who and what I AM, I have done terrible things to the people, places, and things in my experience.

What I Give, I Live. When I give people, places, and things my hate, anger, and frustration, I Live my hate, anger, and frustration in that moment and I have set the stage for it to return in future moments.

Yes, my deepest heartfelt most secret beliefs always come back.

What I Give, I Live. Whatever my deepest heartfelt most secret beliefs are they always come to the surface of my experience. I Give the essence of my being to people, places, and things; bad or Good, sad or Happy, hateful or Loving, hole or Whole, incomplete or Complete.

There is no punishment in the experience of God, but there are consequences to my Choices. My Choices access the Limitless Potential of God and allow me to experience whatever I believe with all my heart, mind, and being.

Do I enjoy my experience of pain over Abundant Joy?

Whatever I Experience, I AM Choosing, and only I can Change my experience. Until I accept that I Create my experience in all its myriad of forms, I fight with what shows up in my life. When I fight with what is in my life, I AM Choosing to Create and Accept pain over finding a path that Creates and Accepts Abundant Joy from All That Is.

Only I can Choose to play with frustrating toys.

It is my Choice to believe that I must be right. Whenever, I must be right, my emotionally guided opinions (ego) will fight to be just that because it believes I win through being right or I lose through being wrong.

God Giving Ongoing Direction says I can be, do, or have anything just for the experience of it and that I can make a new Choice in my experience of All That Is, whenever I AM ready.

Do I realize that I AM the Co-Creator?
I AM Love and Compassion.
I AM the instigator.

Everything I experience, I have Chosen. When my experience is far from what I desire, I can Choose again. The Limitless Potential of God allows me to Choose always in all ways.

I AM the instigator of all my experience. I have instigated hate and frustration, and I have instigated Love and Compassion. It is always my Choice. My Choice is the Conscious Creative Cycle in my life.

I AM LOVE AND COMPASSION

Everything I experience, I have Chosen. When my experience is far from what I desire, I can Choose again. The Limitless Potential of God allows me to Choose always in all ways.

Celebration of Love Vows

I wrote this last chapter as a Celebration of Love for my Intimate Relationship.

I present it here with the Intention that it can be used for the Celebration of Love by any two (or more) people Consciously Choosing to join as a Loving Lasting Union of an adult intimate Relationship or a Conscious Community.

Please use it as it is, or use it as an inspiration to adapt for your own loving vows.

Celebration of Love Vows

Spiritual Leader:
(Spiritual Leader welcomes everyone)

____ and ____ (and ____) have come here on this day to make public their commitment of love, out of their desire that we all come to feel a very real and Intimate part of their decision, for where two or more are gathered the will of Love, Life, and God is powerfully evoked.

____ and ____ (and ____) hope that this experience of bonding will help to bring us all closer together. Please let this celebration be a rededication of your own loving bond with all of life.

____ and ____ (and ____) have put a lot of thought and energy into their celebration of love. They believe that all their personal choices allow them to Authentically Experience and Joyfully Express the Grandest Feeling of God through their beings.

____ and ____ (and ____) wish now, that their most cherished intentions of Love and Commitment be shared and affirmed for this celebration.

This is a celebration of Love and Light and shadow and Family. The candles around the room represent the Love and Light present in everything. During this Celebration of Love today, let the Light within your being, join with the Light of all around you. Let the shadows brought forth from our combined Light be a reminder of our greatest shared opportunities for Wholeness provided through the Love and Acceptance of all our Light and shadow. Please let all opportunities, which are powerfully mirrored to us through our world family be healing.

(Spiritual Leader turns to ____ and ____ (and ____))

___ and ___ (and ___), you have explained to me that you have come here today with the firm understanding that the Love of God resides within you and flows through you, as it does through all of life . . . that you join together consciously choosing to open all your love, all your wisdom, all your insight, all your knowledge, all your understanding, all your strength, all your passion, all your compassion, and all your vulnerability to be fully engaged in your Relationship with each other and all of life.

Is God's Presence still your guiding Love in your commitment?

___ and ___ (and ___):
It is.

Spiritual Leader:
You have also told me that it is your belief that you are entering your commitment to experience and express

your Grandest Feeling of Light and Freedom . . . you choose to support each other as you genuinely express your deeply heartfelt honest celebrations of Love and Joy with others . . . You choose your personal boundaries rather than imposing your personal choices . . . you wish for all your relations that they open up to their shadows and follow their Light to inner peace and world peace . . . you freely share all that you be, do, and have; including your Love of God, your Love of people, your Love of life, your Love of work, your Love of play, your Love of abundance, and your Love of transformation with each other and all of life.

Is Freedom still your fullest expression of Light through your commitment?

____ and ____ (and ____):
It is.

Spiritual Leader:

You have shared with me that your commitment provides you with the greatest opportunity for spiritual growth and emotional healing . . . that you are Intimate mirrors for the shadows you create with your light ... that only through the expression and reception of your deepest feelings can your intimacy flourish . . . in your times of acceptance and especially in your times of denial . . . and through your shadow, you choose to heal as you fully express your soul's deepest yearnings with each other and all of life.

Is your shadow still your greatest gift within your commitment?

___ and ___ (and ___):
It is.

Spiritual Leader:

Finally, your Celebration of Love today bonds

together a family. In your family, you recognize The Love of God as your centre, you choose Light and Freedom as your natural expression, and you believe your shadow provides powerful opportunities for your family to create Wholeness and Unity with all of Love, Life, and God. In your family, you choose to provide a stable and structured atmosphere that encourages open discussions, fosters emotional expressions, and supports vulnerable interactions for all the caring souls involved and for all the souls within your care.

Is family still your covenant within your commitment?

___ and ___ (and ___):

It is.

The rings are shown
Spiritual Leader:
A circle is the symbol of the cyclical nature of life, of

the scared hoop, of the sun, the earth, and the Universe. A circle is the symbol of Universal Unity. The Oneness of all things within the Being of God. The eternal spiritual truth of all, without beginning or end.

___ and ___ (and ___) choose this symbol to represent their Love and Understanding of Being One with God, Freedom, Opportunity, and Family.

Now, ___ and ___ (and ___), please place your hands over these rings; your symbols of love and commitment.

They place their hands over the rings

Spiritual Leader:
___ and ___ (and ___), please repeat after me: . . . I consciously choose . . . to be your friend, your lover, and your nurturing partner . . . I announce and declare

my intention . . . to give our Relationship . . . my deepest friendship and love . . . when our moments are high . . . and when they are low . . .when we express our Light . . . and when we express our shadow . . . when we act with Love . . . and when we act from fear . . . when our energy is clouded . . . and when our energy is clear . . . I announce to all of Love, Life, and God . . . that I choose to always seek . . . our Light of Divinity . . . especially when our shadow . . . comes into our shared destiny. . . It is my intention to be joined as one . . . in a holy union of our souls . . . that we may be God in expression . . . sharing all that is loving, healing, and nurturing within us . . . with all whose lives help make us Whole . . . We Are One with God . . . We Are One with the world . . . We Are One.

Spiritual Leader:

Please take hold of your rings, these symbols of your love . . . give them a place upon your hands . . . and repeat after me . . . With these rings, We Consciously Bless . . . so that all may know of the Love within us. The only power that can truly grant the declaration that these souls have shared today is the Light within their own souls. Only they can create their experience. However, they are grateful that we have chosen to witness and support their declaration on this day.

So now, inasmuch as you, ___, and you, ___, (and you, ___,) have announced the truth written in your hearts, and have expressed this truth in the presence of these, your family, your friends, and the Light of God in all things . . . we Joyfully observe that you have declared yourselves to be joined as friends, lovers, and nurturing partners.

Let us pray.

Spirit of Love and Life. These souls have declared that their destinies are now One design, that Your Light is central to their lives and informs their entire experience, and that Your Freedom enhances their opportunities for growth and healing in their shared experience of each other, of family, and within the world.

___ and ___ (and ___), may all your relations be constantly enriched by the beauty and bounty of your love for all. May all your creations express the Joyous Feeling of God through you for the world. May your hearts and home be a place of love, nurturing, growth, and happiness for all who enter; a place where young and old are cherished in each other's presence; a place of music, art, laughter, and tears; a place of prayer, joy, passion, and cheers; and may your place be one of the Love of God, the Light of Freedom, the Opportunity of Shadows to all in Our World Family, and may your days be good and long and richly blessed upon the Earth. Amen.

I now invite you to seal this with a kiss.

ABOUT THE AUTHOR

Barry Thomas Bechta is an artist, author, and film maker whose work centers around the concepts of Unconditional Love. Barry knew he wanted to write from a very young age and was encouraged with his artistic skills and only began writing full time in his thirties. He wrote his first book, *I AM Creating My Own Experience* as a personal journal to choose connection with God/Life/Energy. He has since written 17 inspirational spiritual books.

Barry loves to hear from people whom have connected with his writing and used it as a tool to improve their lives. If you would like to write him about your personal experiences as a result of reading any of his books, Barry encourages you to do so.

You can also get a Free Digital Copy of *I AM Creating My Own Experience - The Creation Vibration* from his main website:

www.unconditionallovebooks.com

Unconditional Love Books Titles of Related Interest
by Barry Thomas Bechta

I AM Creating My Own Experience
978-0-9813485-5-1

I AM Creating My Own Answers
978-0-9686835-1-4

I AM Creating My Own Dreams
978-0-9686835-2-1

I AM Creating My Own Relationships
978-0-9686835-3-8

I AM Creating My Own Abundance
978-0-9686835-4-5

I AM Creating My Own Success
978-0-9686835-5-2

I AM Creating My Own Happiness
978-0-9686835-6-9

I AM Creating My Own Experience - The Creation Vibration
978-0-9686835-7-6

I AM Creating My Own Experience - To Manifest Money
978-0-9686835-8-3

I AM Creating My Own Experience - 369 Conscious Days
978-0-9686835-9-0

Loving Oneness
978-0-9813485-0-6

Trust Life
978-0-9813485-1-3

I AM Creating My Own Financial Freedom - The Story
978-0-9813485-2-0

I AM Creating My Own Financial Freedom - The Lessons
978-0-9813485-3-7

Laughing Star's Guide to Laughter, Life, Love, and God
978-0-9813485-4-4

All of the above are books are available through your local bookstore, or they may be ordered as digital downloads at
www.unconditionallovebooks.com

Barry Thomas Bechta is available for interviews, special events, workshops, and lectures that redefine, guide, and inspire everyone's connection to the Creative Power within themselves. To arrange author interviews, special events, workshops, or lectures, please contact:

**UNCONDITIONAL
LOVE BOOKS**

**Unconditional Love Books
Box # 610 - 2527 Pine St.,
Vancouver, BC, Canada V6J 3E8**

info@unconditionallovebooks.com

www.unconditionallovebooks.com

For additional copies of Barry's books, products, and services please contact your local book seller. Many products and services are Only available to order directly from the publisher as eProducts on the website.

Thanks for your purchase and Remember to Consciously Create your Life.

Right Now is the Only Moment of Creation

Enjoy it Fully!